DON'T BRING ME DOWN

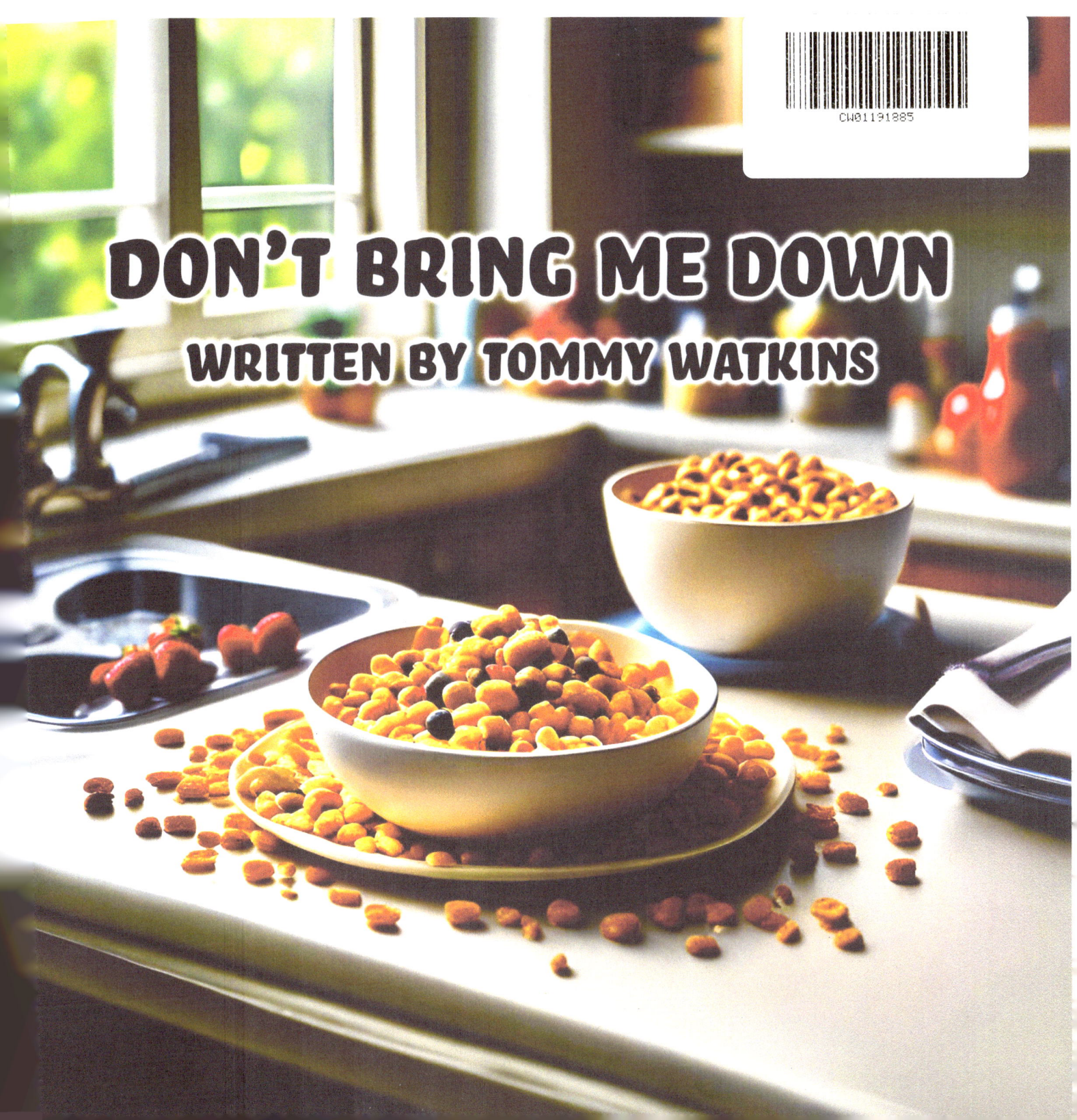

WRITTEN BY TOMMY WATKINS

Saturday had come. The sun was shining bright in the neighborhood.

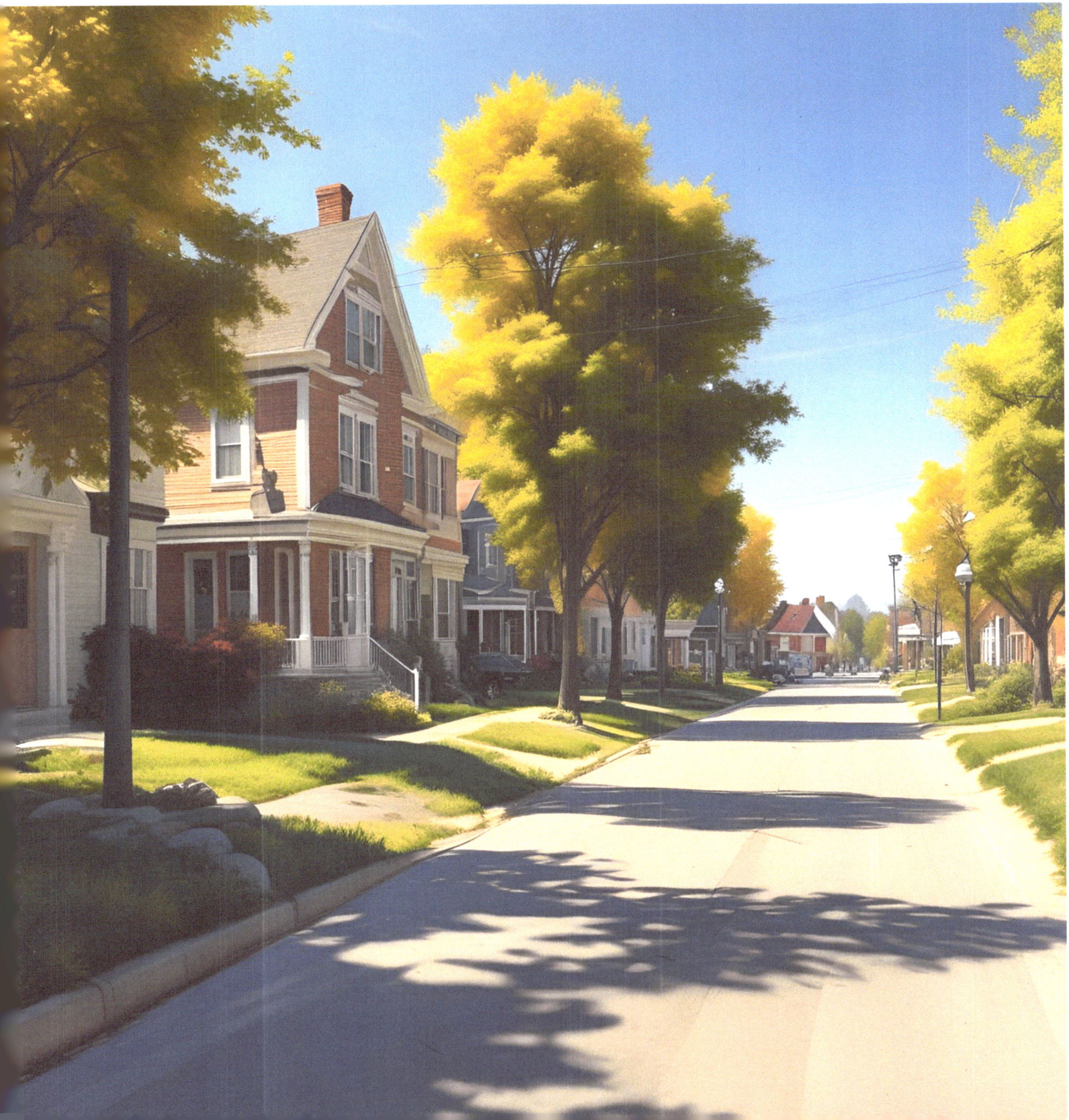

The two boys woke up, had breakfast, and ate their favorite cereal.

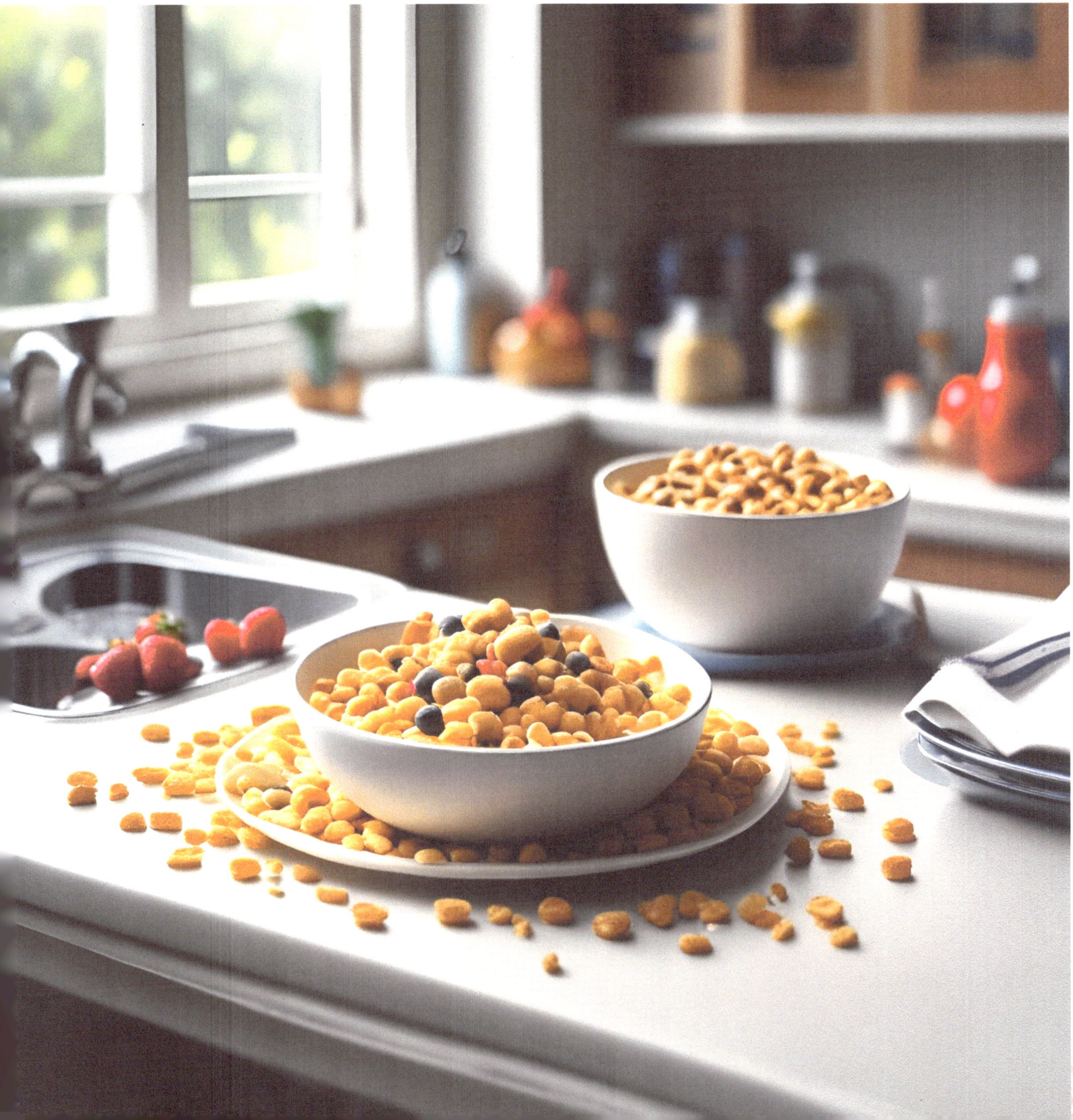

Watching their favorite cartoons, they enjoy the morning.

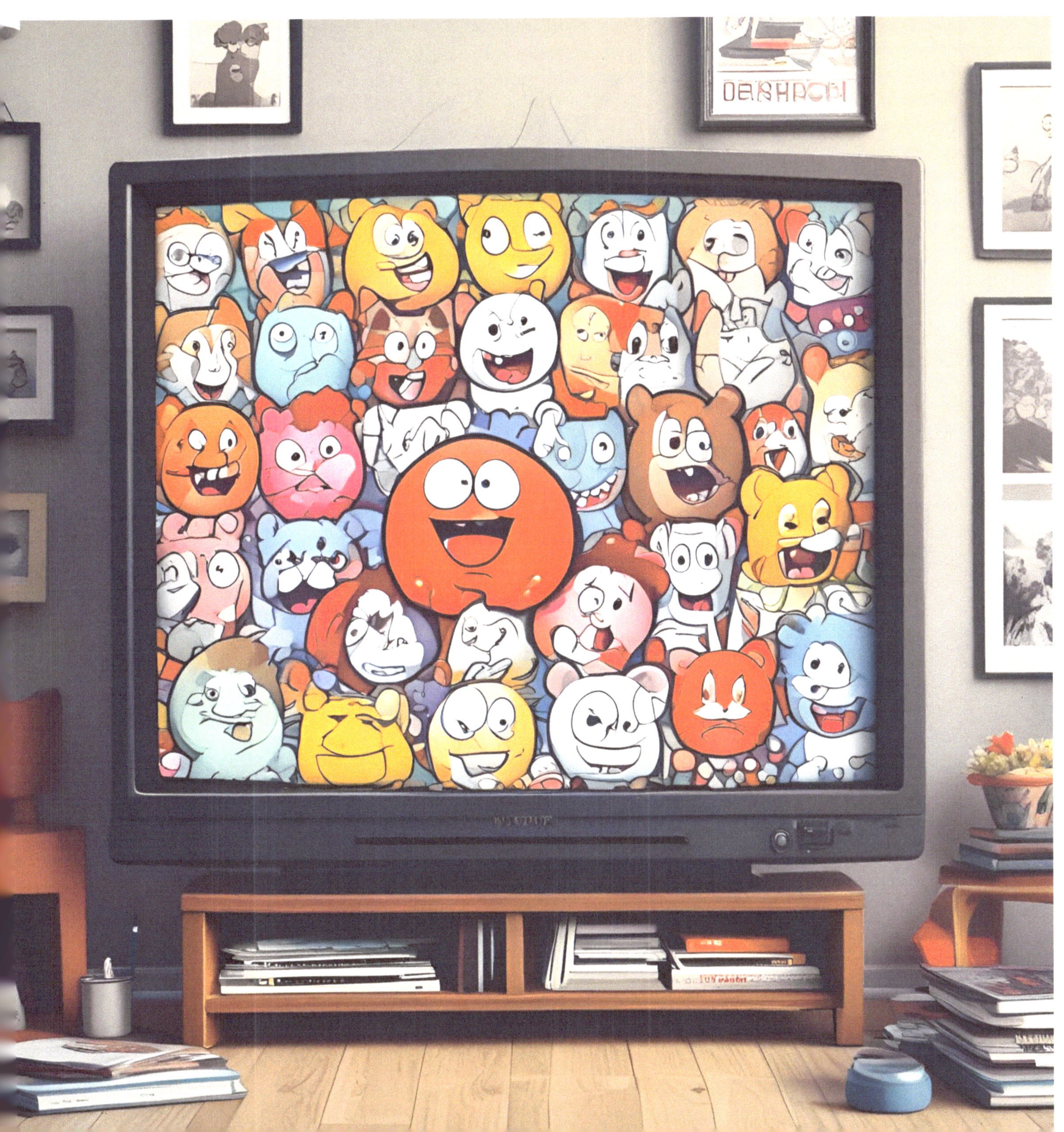

The boys go outside and start mowing the yard, raking, and doing other outside work.

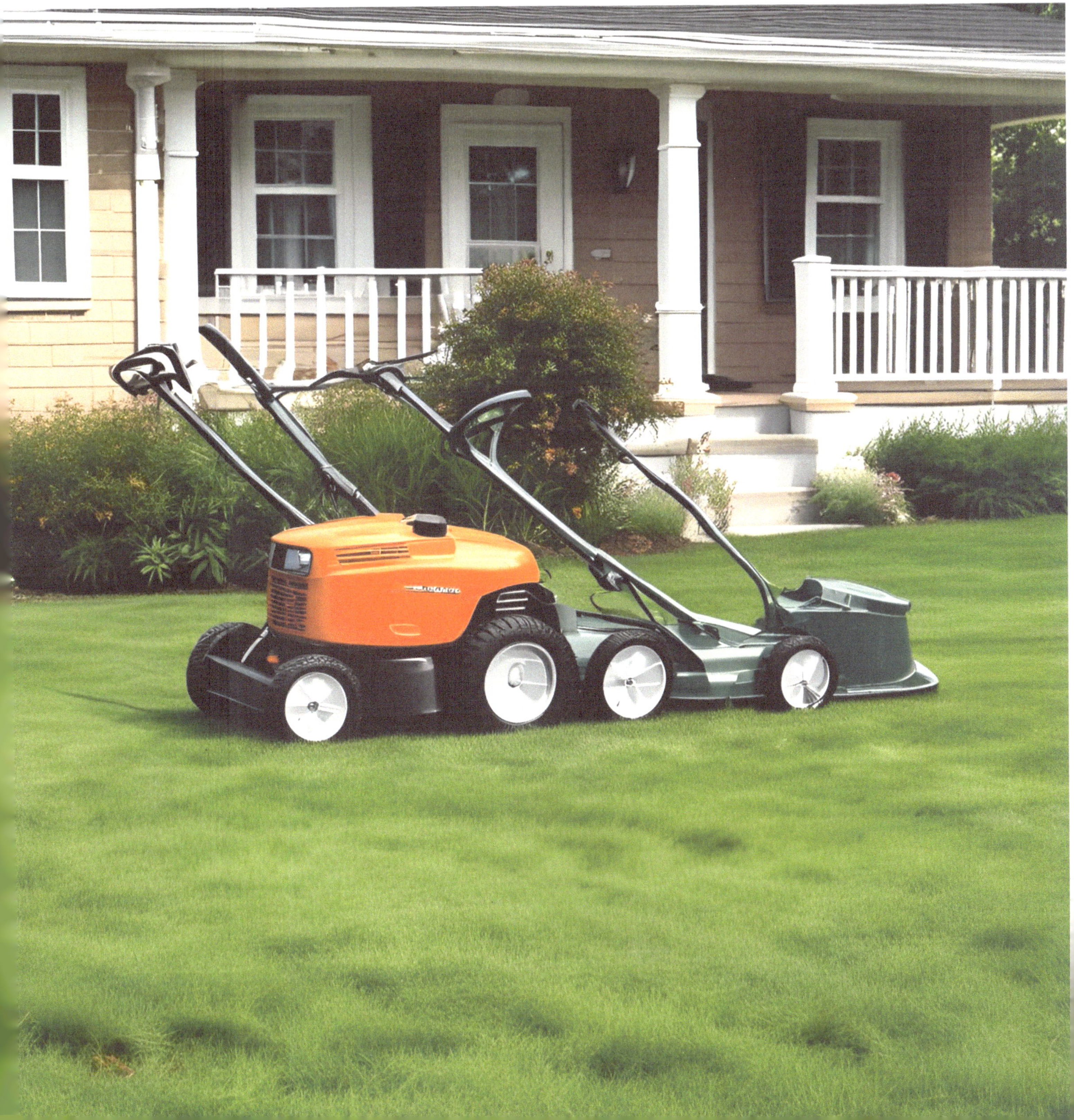

Dad starts a fire of leaves and mowed grass. The boys are finishing up. Mom starts the BBQ for dinner.

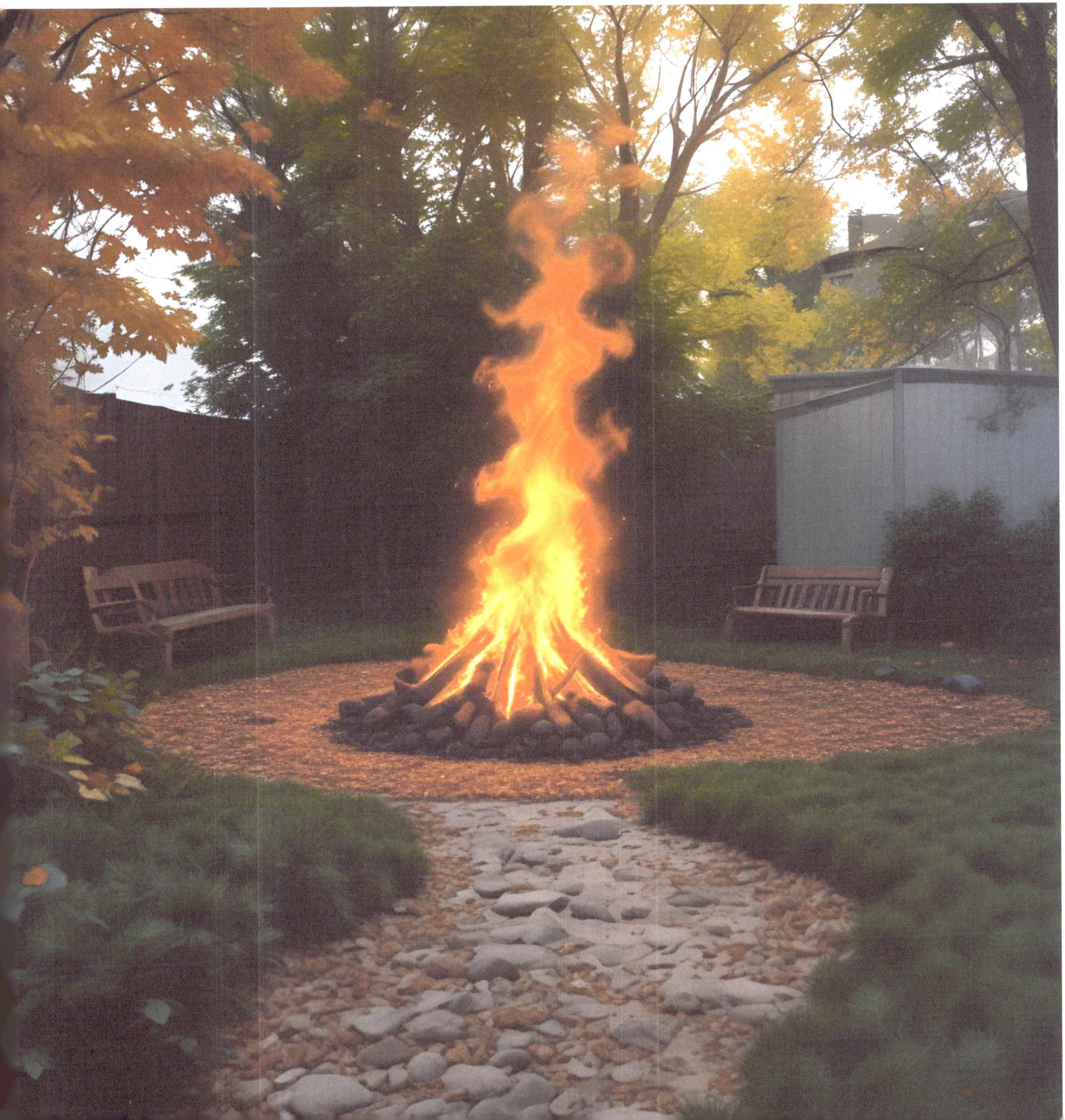

The work is finished for the day. The boys hang out by the fire with a soda.

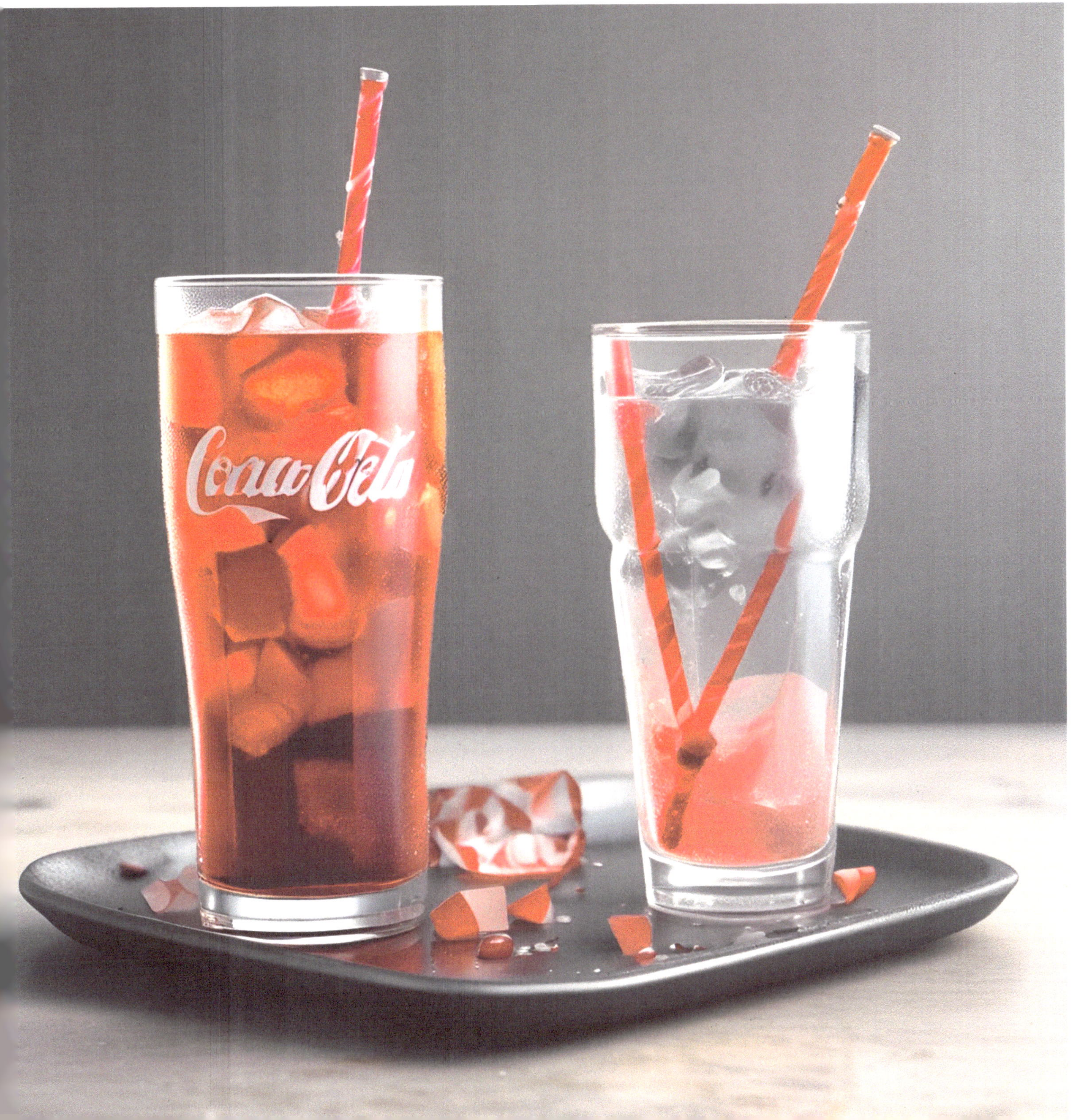
Coca-Cola

The fire dies down, and they go inside to play video games before dinner.

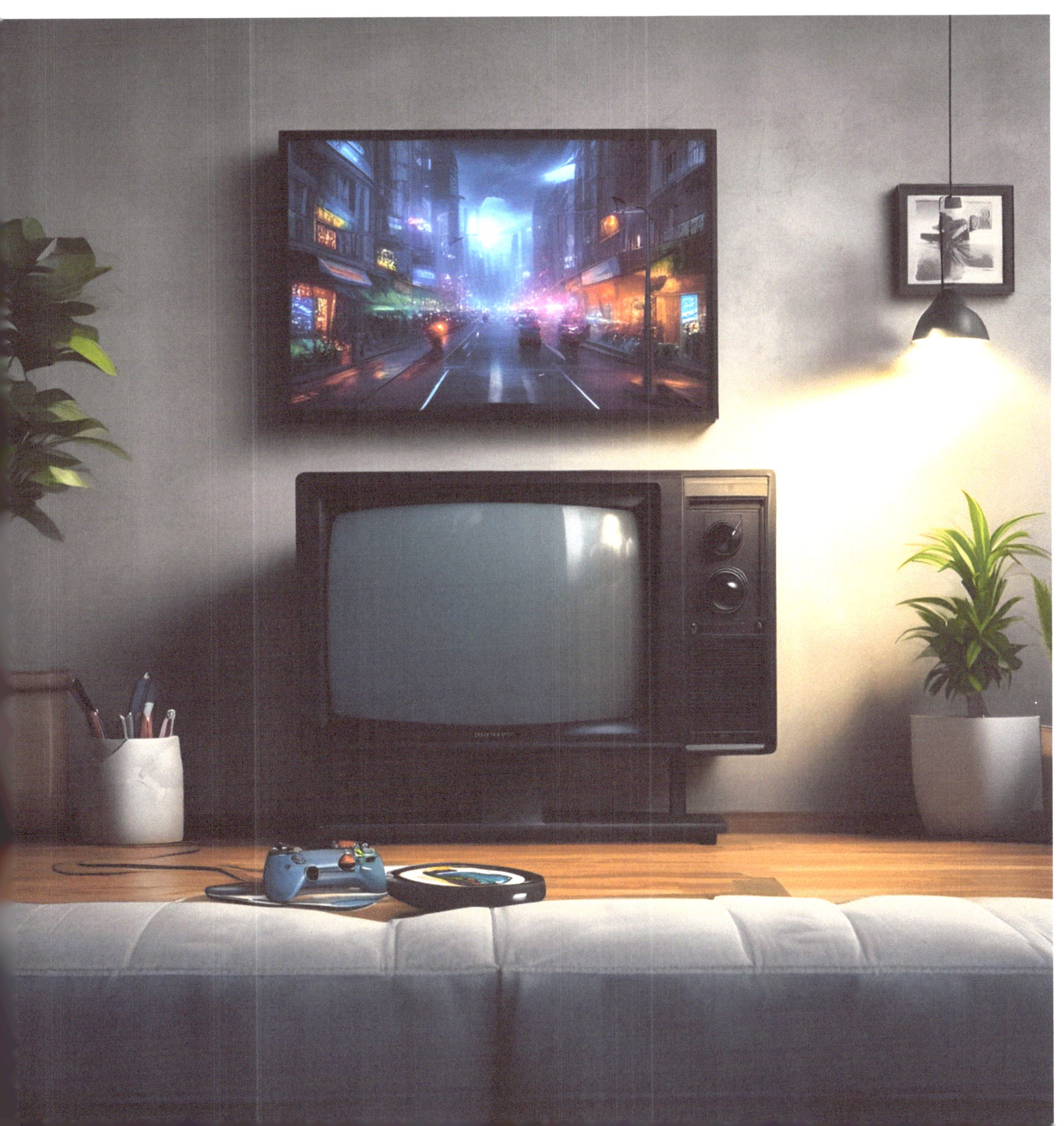

As dinner is cooking, the boys go outside and play a game of street hockey.

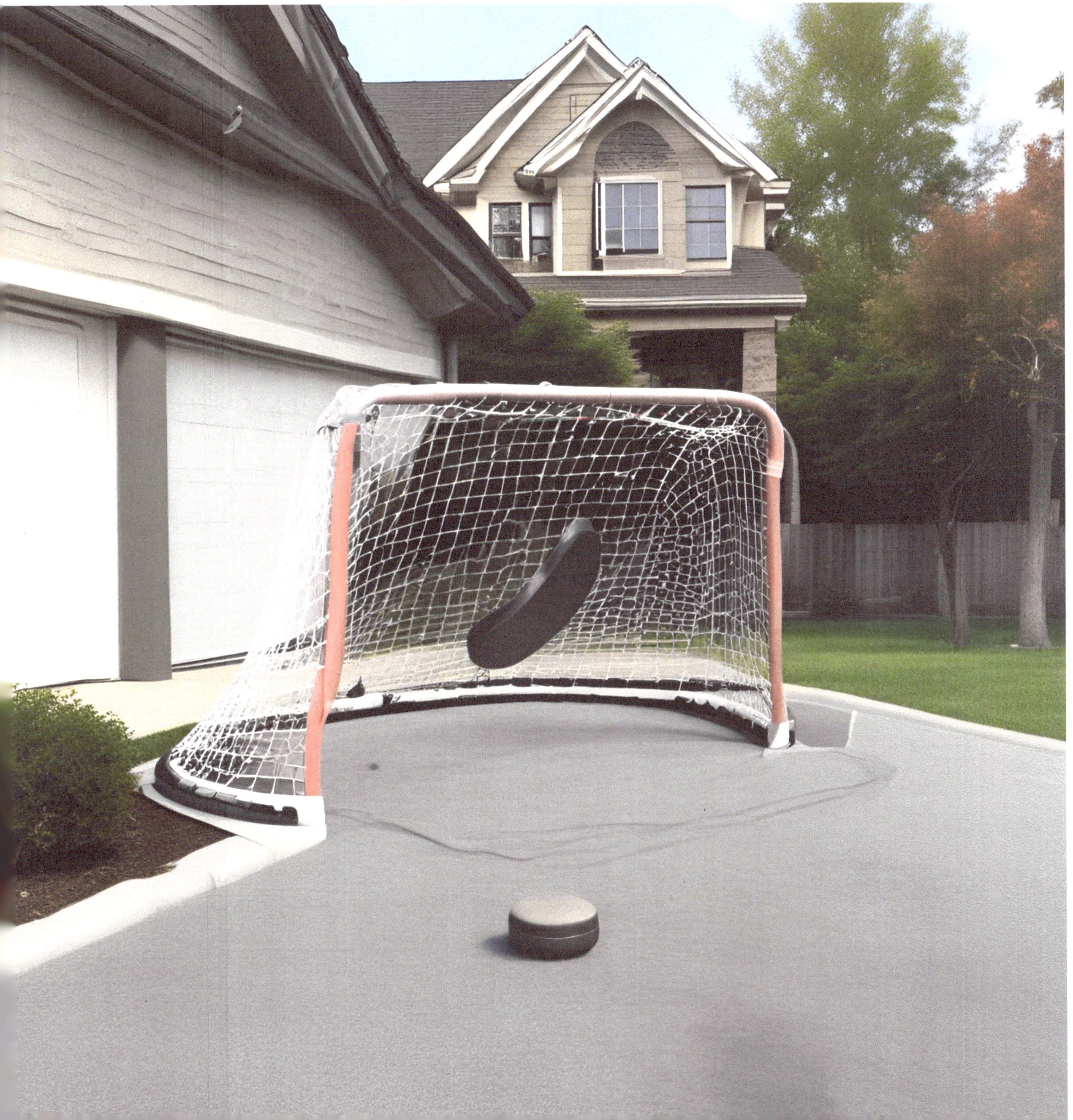

The cheeseburgers and hot dogs are of the grill, and the family gathers for dinner. They sit outside and enjoy dinner on the patio.

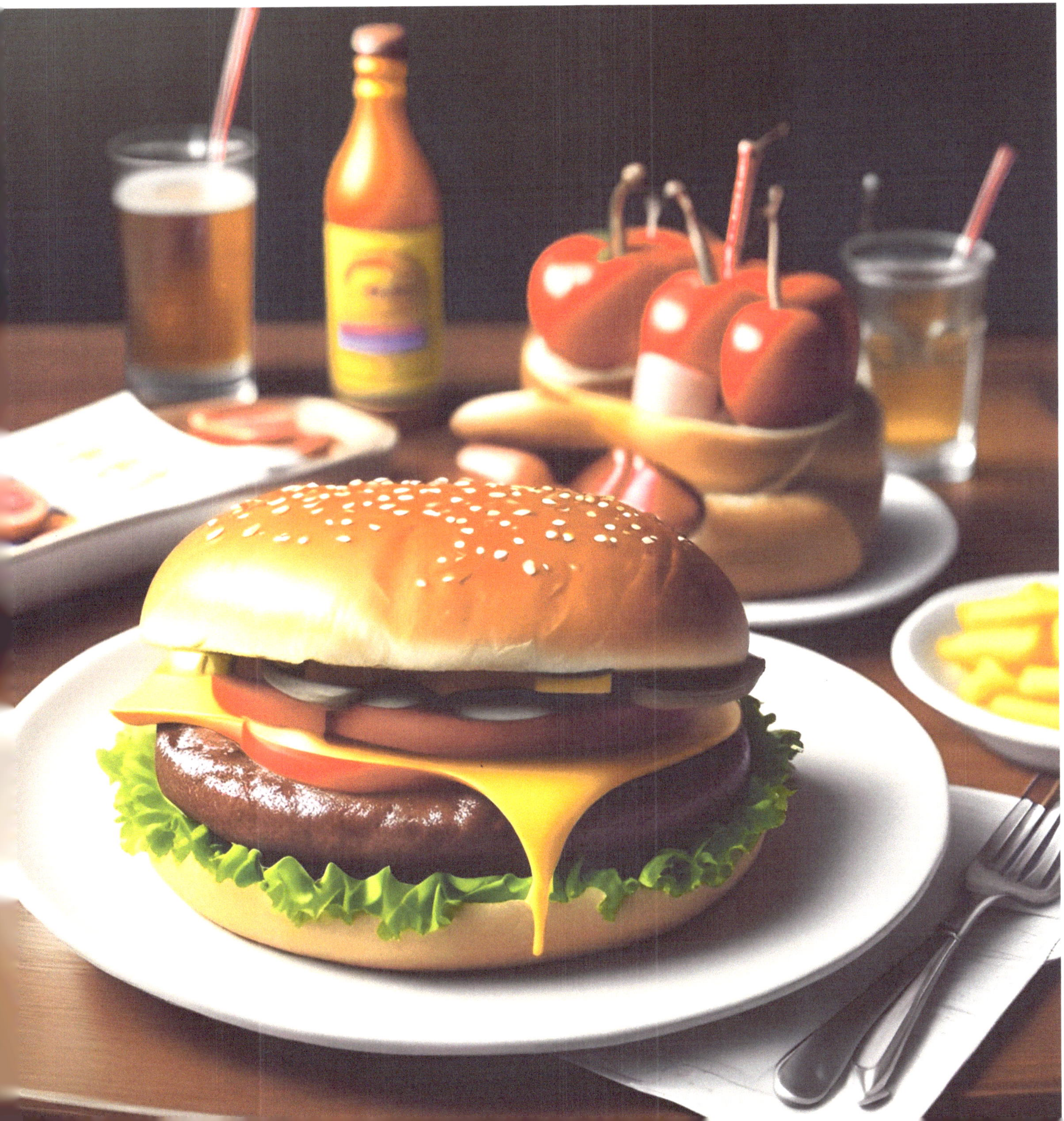

Dinner ends with a great movie on the television.

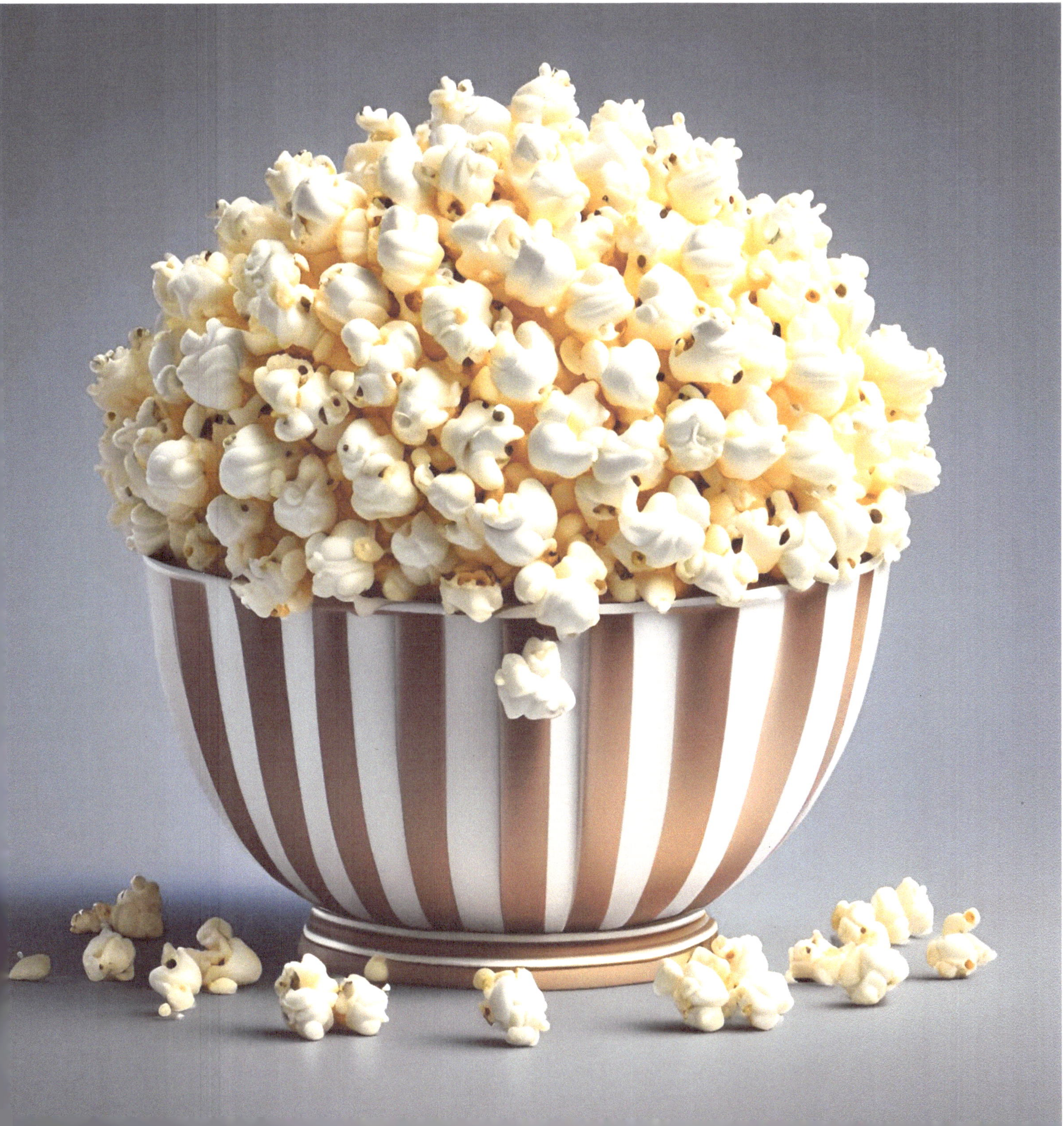

The night ends with the family going to bed. The family had a perfect day.

The End